Listen to your HEART

A LINE-A-DAY JOURNAL

Karen Salmansohn

Illustrated by Miriam Bos

Andrews McMeel
PUBLISHING®

this journal belongs to

INTRODUCTION

We live in a world of constant noise. So many things battling for our attention: People. Work. Texts. News. Social media. Netflix. Oh my!

It's no wonder so many of us feel overwhelmed—and confused about what steps we need to take to feel happier and more loved.

We haven't been prioritizing taking time to listen to our heart.

Meanwhile, our heart has lots of helpful, life-boosting insights to share with us.

But silly us. We haven't been paying attention.

These days, far too many of us spend far too much time . . .

- ♥ Scrolling through news feeds—while our heart goes unfed
- ♥ Checking who's following us—rather than following our heart
- ♥ Or recharging our phone—but not our spirit

The solution?

We need to take time to sit in silence and chitchat with our heart.

In fact, I believe we can greatly deepen and lengthen our happiness by taking a little time each day to eavesdrop on what our heart's been trying to tell us.

I know, I know. You might be wondering how the heck you're gonna find time to sit and listen to your heart? After all, you're a very busy person—with an already overstuffed schedule.

So I have a time-thrifty solution!

I want you to swap out one text a day on your phone—and trade it for one line a day in this journal!

Yep, in the two minutes it takes you to send a single text on your phone, you can instead scribble down a single sentence in this journal.

The benefits you reap will be enormous:
- ♥ Improvements in your intuition
- ♥ Insights to help your various relationships
- ♥ Creative ideas to improve your work
- ♥ Gratitude for your blessings
- ♥ Self-awareness for what you need to change
- ♥ Self-love for all your awesomeness
- ♥ Greater confidence in making the right decisions
- ♥ Needed attention to whatever you've been avoiding/ignoring
- ♥ Brilliant ideas for making and saving more money
- ♥ Lowered anxiety and boosted calm
- ♥ Lessons learned and forgiveness released

Basically, if you want to live a rich, full, happy life, you need to take time for regular tough-love chats with your heart.

This line-a-day journal will help you to do just that!

Enjoy!

xo, Karen

**Talk about your blessings
more than your problems.
What are you grateful for?**

There's a big difference between a TO-DO LIST and a TO-DO-WHAT-MATTERS-MOST LIST. What matters most right now?

Don't focus on what's going wrong. Focus on what's going right. What are you proud about right now?

Life is too short to stress about people who don't deserve room in your heart. Name 6 people you trust and cherish.

1.

2.

3.

4.

5.

6.

Go for your dreams.
Don't be a wuss.
What step can you take
to move forward?

Who was the last person you texted?
Describe something you appreciate about this person.

List 3 things you're grateful about. Then go back and underline these 3 things and put exclamation marks after them—to remind yourself to stay grateful.

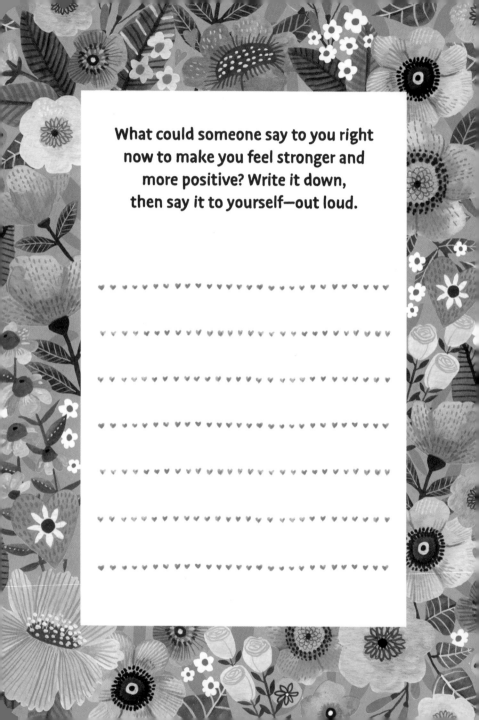

What could someone say to you right now to make you feel stronger and more positive? Write it down, then say it to yourself—out loud.

List 3 things that make you smile. Commit on this page to experiencing these things more often.

1.

2.

3.

If you were to write a memoir, what would its title be— and the main plotline?

Describe yourself in 10 words or fewer.

What is your most treasured childhood memory?

What do you need to start saying NO to?

What do you need to start saying YES to?

Draw a happy selfie of yourself.

If you had a song playing as the
soundtrack for your life
during the last week—what
would this song be, and why?

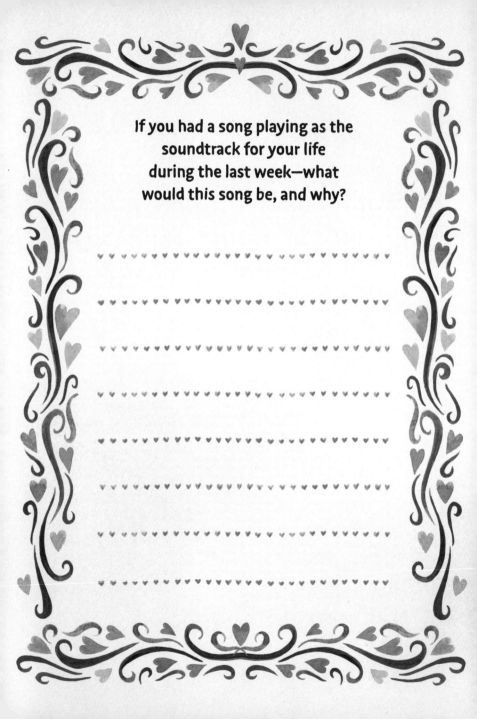

Write a love note to your body.

Describe a time you cried happy tears.

The only real mistake is the one you don't bother to learn from. Share what you learned from a recent mistake.

Listen to your heart and fill in the blank:
"I feel most energized when I . . ."

Be a warrior, not a worrier. Share some convincing reasons you shouldn't worry about whatever's on your mind.

**Write a note to your inner critic—
explaining that they are fired. Buh-bye!**

Share a goal you hope to accomplish this year.

What do you feel you have
true talent doing? Brag a little.
Make yourself blush.

Develop supersonic inner hearing. Take a moment to listen to your heart's quiet whisperings. Ask yourself a question of your choice. Close your eyes. Get quiet for 20 seconds. Write down your answer.

Share a happy memory of a family member
who's been there for you during tough times.
Reenergize your heart with appreciation and love.

💜💜

_____

_____

_____

_____

_____

💜💜

_____

People are always "telling" you things without words—
things you need to perk up and pay attention to.
Listen to your heart. What do you need to know about
someone—that you might not want to know?

Share a compliment people have told you about yourself.
Take a moment to revel in these kind words.

**Listen to your heart and fill in the blank:
"I know I'm going to get through
this challenge because . . ."**

Who is one of your role models?
Why do they inspire you?

What movie do you feel relates to you/your life the most? Why?

....

....

....

....

....

....

....

Name something you look forward to happening this month.

Write a love note to your younger self.

Write a love note to your future self.

❤❤

_____

_____

_____

_____

_____

                                              ❞❞

_____

What's a core value that you are highly passionate
about maintaining? Listen to your heart,
and be sure to regularly embrace this core value.

What's something very few people know about you?

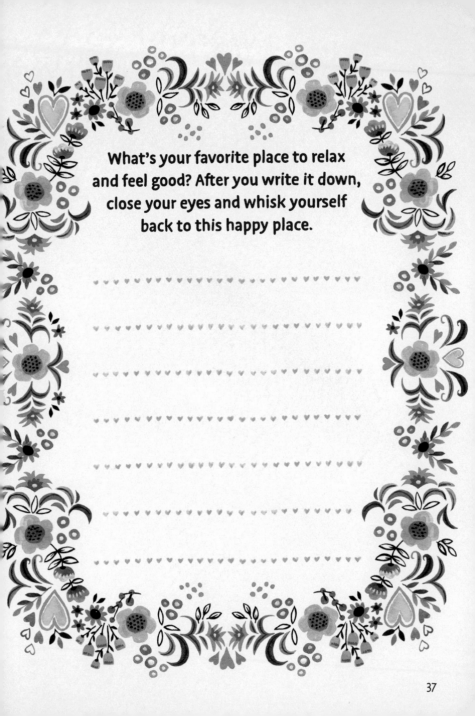

What's your favorite place to relax and feel good? After you write it down, close your eyes and whisk yourself back to this happy place.

Share a time you felt proud of yourself.

Your heart wants you to lighten up—and let go
of what's weighing you down. What's something you
need to forgive yourself for? Forgive yourself now.

Weird is the new awesome. Celebrate your weirdness in a few words.

What's a life lesson you learned the hard, bumpy, twisty-turn way? Remember, the past is good to learn from—not live in.

What's a strange coincidence or surprising synchronicity that happened to you—which your heart wants you to perk up and pay attention to?

💜💜

_____

_____

_____

_____

_____

💜💜

_____

Your heart loves to save, store, and treasure beautiful memories. What is your first happy childhood memory?

What do you still own from your childhood— and why did you keep it?

What's the most beautiful place on this planet? After you write it down, close your eyes and beam yourself to this gorgeous location.

Write a little about the best gift you ever received.

Write about the hardest phone call you ever made or received.

What does your heart say you should do differently in your work life?

What does your heart say you should do differently when it comes to your health?

What does your heart say you need to learn from a past relationship?

❤❤

_____

_____

_____

_____

_____

_____

❤❤

_____

What does your heart say about who you need to have a conversation with—that you've been avoiding.

Write about something that happened to you that makes you believe in God or a higher spirit.

Eavesdrop on your heart.
What do you want to have
more of in your life?

Eavesdrop on your heart.
What do you want to have less of in your life?

Who do you go to for the most straight-up honest answers to your most personal questions?

❤️❤️

_____

_____

_____

_____

_____

❤️❤️

_____

List 3 aspects of yourself that you really, really like! Make your heart smile.

**Describe a favorite vacation memory.
After you write it down, close your eyes and
time travel back to this vacation spot.**

Who is the funniest person in your life?
Describe something they said that made you laugh.

Who is the best cook in your life?
Describe their yummiest meal.

**Who is the most generous person in your life?
What act of kindness did they do for you
that you will forever appreciate?**

What are your pet peeves—that make you crazy? How do you handle them?

♥ ♥

♥ ♥

♥ ♥

♥ ♥

♥ ♥

♥ ♥

♥ ♥

♥ ♥

Describe a favorite teacher or mentor.

Jim Rohn says we become like the 5 people we spend the most time with. Who are your 5? How are they affecting you—your behaviors, your thoughts, your life?

❤❤

_____

_____

_____

_____

_____

❞❞

_____

List something you SHOULD do, that you don't want to do. Why?

List something you SHOULD NOT do, that you do. Why?

What core values broke up past friendships?
What can you learn about life and love from this?

💕

_____

_____

_____

_____

_____

💬

_____

What quality do you have to offer in friendships— that is a highly special attribute?

What quality do you have to offer in romance— that is a highly special attribute?

What quality do you
have to offer in business—
that is a highly special attribute?

What was the most amount of money you ever made
for your talent? What trait led to earning it?

What was the work project you've been the proudest of? What unique trait of yours led to its creation?

Whom do you admire?
What can you learn to do more of because of their positive habits?

Whom do you resent? What can you learn to do less of because of their negative habits?

Out of all the people you personally know, who do you think is the happiest? What can you learn from them?

Who do you think has the most balance between their career and personal life? What can you learn from them?

What are some vulnerable negative triggers
that can shoot disruptive holes into a happy day?
Vow to avoid/block these triggers.

What self-talk do you do when you're feeling cocky? After you write it down, repeat it out loud while looking in the mirror.

Given the choice of anyone in the world, whom would you want as a dinner guest . . . and why?

What good qualities do you appreciate in your mother?

What good qualities do you appreciate in your father?

Always trust your heart. If you feel something is wrong, it probably is. Write down something your heart wants you to be on the lookout about.

Intuition isn't about seeing into the future.
It's about seeing into the present. Quiet your mind,
then write down something you intuit.

It's important to know the difference between your intuition guiding you and your limiting beliefs misleading you. Get quiet and share a true intuition.

The best advice you'll ever hear will come from your heart.
Share a little heartfelt advice with yourself now.

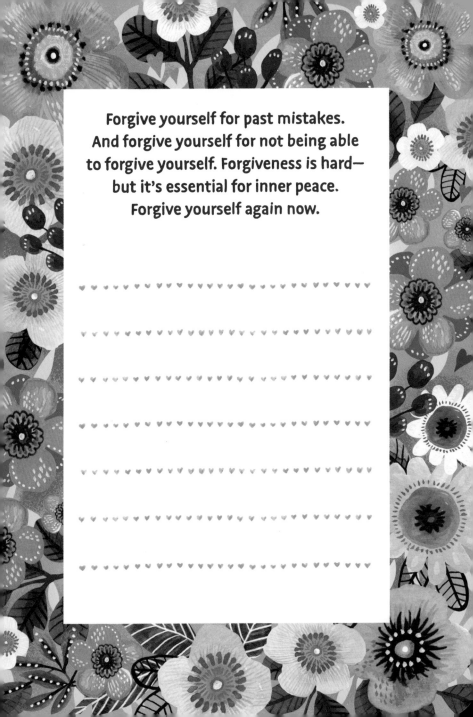

Forgive yourself for past mistakes.
And forgive yourself for not being able
to forgive yourself. Forgiveness is hard—
but it's essential for inner peace.
Forgive yourself again now.

Your heart has a quick reminder: You only get a limited amount of days on this planet. Today is a good day to do something to make yourself happy. Write down something to do that will make you happy.

Don't let a hard lesson harden your heart.
Share how you've grown in the last few years,
thanks to all your experiences.

Hate takes pieces of your heart.
Love brings peace to your heart.
Share a loving thought on this page.

Your heart has a quick reminder: Everything you're going through is preparing you for what you truly need to live your best life. Share a lesson you think you're meant to be learning right now.

Good looks fade. But a good heart keeps you beautiful forever. Share a little something good about yourself.

Be careful not to let the pain of a broken heart lead to the pain of a blocked heart. Commit to letting go of the past and reveling more in the beauty of the here and now.

What's on your mind becomes what's in your life.
So think the thoughts you want to see.
Share a little something you want to manifest.

We need to text less
on the phone and talk more from
our hearts. Who do you need to
have a heart-to-heart talk with?
What do you need to say?

Listen to your heart. It's reporting daily on issues most important to you! Share a top headline you feel your heart is presently trying to report about!

Your heart has a quick reminder: People who have passed away still hold a special place in your heart. Share a happy memory of someone who passed.

Warning: Your thoughts are either poison or nourishment to your heart. Write down a nourishing thought.

Your heart has a quick reminder: Endings
are awesome new beginnings in disguise.
Share an example of how the end of something
brought you to the start of something better.

Counting blessings multiplies your happiness.
Count 3 blessings now!

❤❤

_____

_____

_____

_____

_____

❞❤

_____

Your heart has a quick reminder: When things feel like they're not working out, focus on what's working right. Share something awesomely right on this page.

It's time to move on! (Pssst . . . Whatever you thought of when you read those words, write about in a sentence—and know that it's going to be okay.)

Your heart has a quick reminder:
Doing good not only feels good—
it leads to more good. What's
something good you can do?

Being happy is not about getting the best of everything, but making the best of everything. How can you make the best of a situation you're dealing with right now?

You can't control how some people will treat you—
or what they'll say. But you can control how you
react to it. Share the best way to respond
to a challenging person in your life.

Take a moment to appreciate how
awesome you are. Yeah, YOU!

Watch out for blessing blockers: fear, anger, doubt, jealousy, negative people. Write down these words—then cross out each of them in symbolism of letting them go.

Detoxes are not just for the body. You need to detox your thoughts. What negative beliefs do you need to let go of?

Sometimes it's tough to tell the difference between "I need to save money!" and "You only live once!" Take a moment to get clear on how you might budget better.

Self-care is not selfish. It's self-loving.
How might you pamper yourself more?

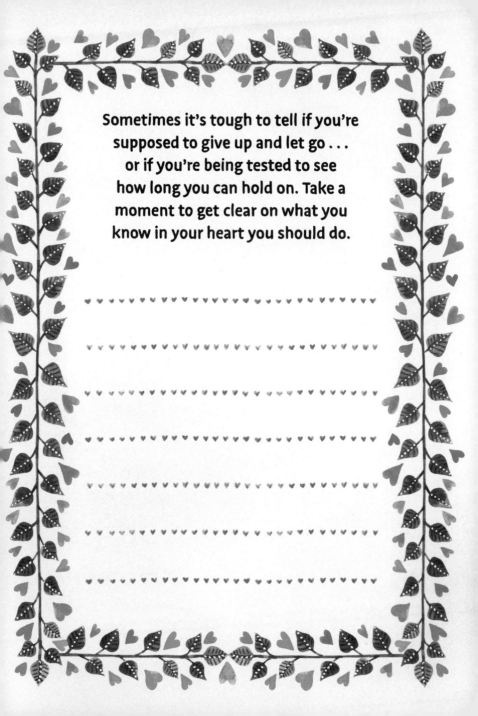

Sometimes it's tough to tell if you're supposed to give up and let go . . . or if you're being tested to see how long you can hold on. Take a moment to get clear on what you know in your heart you should do.

Sometimes a miracle arrives as a small shift—and not a full-blown change. Name a tiny change that has recently happened—which you need to appreciate more.

Don't worry if someone doesn't like you.
Most people are struggling to like themselves.
Name 3 things you like about yourself now.

_____

_____

_____

_____

_____

_____

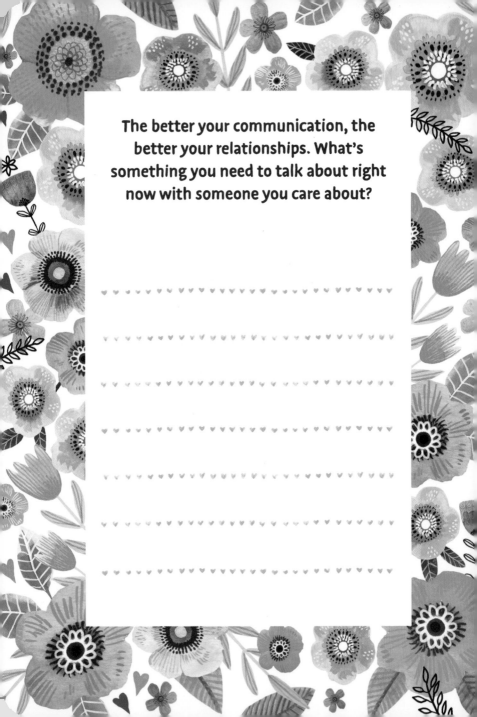

The better your communication, the better your relationships. What's something you need to talk about right now with someone you care about?

Sometimes when bad things happen, we learn to appreciate good things in a whole new light. What's something you need to appreciate more?

Good things are coming. Just keep believing.
Write a positive affirmation now.

_____

_____

_____

_____

_____

_____

When you can't control what's happening, challenge yourself to control the way you respond to or interpret what's happening. That's where your true power is. Tap into this power now.

It doesn't matter if you've failed at something. All that matters is that you get up, dust yourself off, and keep trying. Commit in words that you'll keep trying.

Feel like you're juggling too many things in your day? Get clear on your priorities and values. Vow to become a choosier choice chooser.

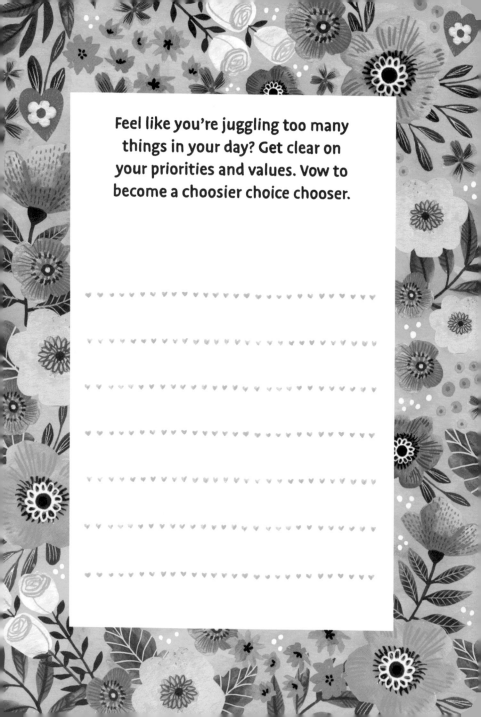

Stop wasting precious energy thinking about what you do not want. Focus that energy on creating the life you do want. Focus some of that energy right here, right now.

**Stop being available for people and things
that make you feel crappy. Vow to stop now.**

In order to be happy, you must let go of the story you thought life would be and find joy in the story you are living. Take a moment to celebrate your life story.

We all choose to receive love and joy at the level of our self-love and self-esteem. If you love yourself a little harder, life will get a lot better. Share something you love about yourself.

Congratulations! You've handled every challenge that's come your way—and grown from things that could have broken you. Celebrate how strong you are.

Taking no action is an action. If you do nothing to move forward toward your dreams, you're still doing something. You're making the choice to stay in the same place. Is that the choice you really want?

**Train your mind to find the good in every situation.
Flex your positivity muscles now.**

Speak your truth. Do not make people guess what you think and how you feel. What do you need to speak up about—and to whom?

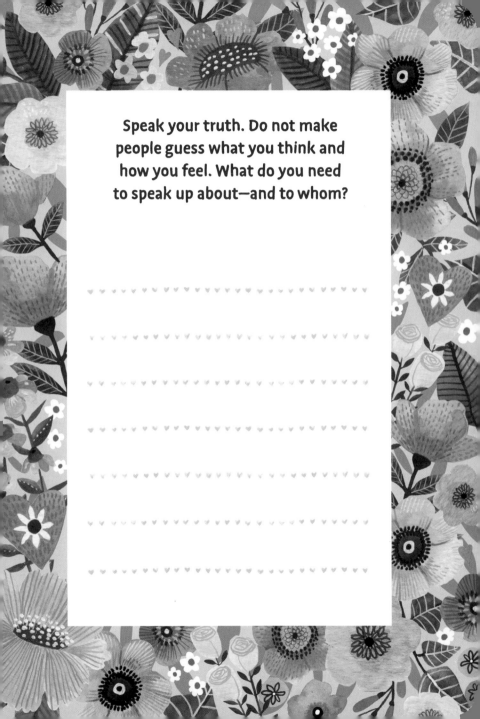

You will be okay. So please don't wait
for things to change to feel okay. Feel okay now.
Okay? Write the word "okay" to commit!

Examine what you tolerate. What you put up with, you end up with. What you allow continues. Reevaluate the costs and your worth.

**Fear works like inter-fear. Share something
you will be braver about—starting today.**

Andrews McMeel Publishing
a division of Andrews McMeel Universal
1130 Walnut Street, Kansas City, Missouri 64106

www.andrewsmcmeel.com

20 21 22 23 24 SDB 10 9 8 7 6 5 4 3 2 1

ISBN: 978-1-5248-5566-6

Editor: Patty Rice
Art Director/Designer: Julie Barnes
Production Editor: Meg Daniels
Production Manager: Tamara Haus

ATTENTION: SCHOOLS AND BUSINESSES
Andrews McMeel books are available at quantity discounts with
bulk purchase for educational, business, or sales promotional use.
For information, please e-mail the Andrews McMeel Publishing
Special Sales Department: specialsales@amuniversal.com.